Caribbean Primary Agriculture

Workbook for infants

R. Ramharacksingh

Illustrated by G. J. Galsworthy

UNIVERSITY PRESS

This is my Agriculture Workbook

My name is _____

I am __ years of age

I am in _____ class

The name of my school is _____

OXFORD
UNIVERSITY PRESS

Great Clarendon Street, Oxford, OX2 6DP, United Kingdom

Oxford University Press is a department of the University of Oxford.
It furthers the University's objective of excellence in research, scholarship,
and education by publishing worldwide. Oxford is a registered trade mark of
Oxford University Press in the UK and in certain other countries

Text © R. Ramharacksingh 1981

The moral rights of the authors have been asserted

First published in 1981 by Cassell
Reprinted by Nelson Thornes Ltd
This edition published by Oxford University Press in 2014

British Library Cataloguing in Publication Data
Data available

978-0-7487-6934-6

20 19 18 17

MIX
Paper from
responsible sources
FSC
www.fsc.org   FSC® C007785

Printed in Great Britain by Bell and Bain Ltd., Glasgow

Acknowledgements
Page make-up: D.P. Media

Although we have made every effort to trace and contact all copyright
holders before publication this has not been possible in all cases. If
notified, the publisher will rectify any errors or omissions at the earliest
opportunity.

Links to third party websites are provided by Oxford in good faith
and for information only. Oxford disclaims any responsibility for
the materials contained in any third party website referenced in
this work.

Books in this series

Level One (5–7 years)
Workbook for infants

Level Two (7–9 years)
Textbook 1   Workbook 1
Textbook 2   Workbook 2

Level Three (9–11 years)
Textbook 3   Workbook 3
Textbook 4   Workbook 4

Living things around us

1 **Write** these words in the spaces below:

die   grow   move

Living things g_____

Living things m_____

Living things d_____

2 Now **colour** the living things below.

3 **Trace** the name of each living thing.

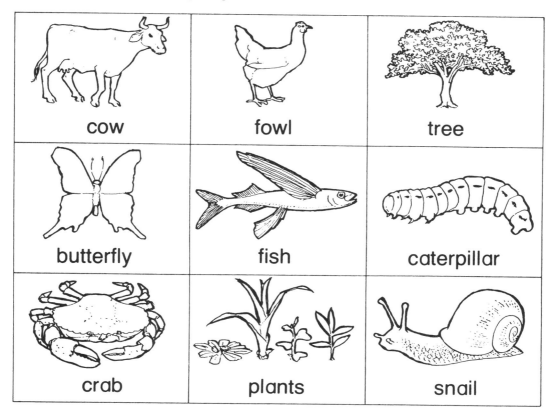

cow	fowl	tree
butterfly	fish	caterpillar
crab	plants	snail

4 Trace this:

Plants and animals are living things.

5 Do this: point out living things around you.

Buildings around us

Here are the names of some buildings.
school   home   farm   grocery   market   factory

1 Now **colour** the buildings below.

2 Write the name below each building.

h__e

s_h__l

f_r_

f__t__y

ma_k_t

g_oc_ry

3 Do this: say what each building is used for.

Land around us

1 **Trace** these:

2 **Colour** these:

This is a hill	
Very high hills are mountains	
Flat lands are called plains	
This is a road	
Here is a river	

3 Trace this:

What is this?
This is a pond

4 Colour this:

People who work in farming

1 Trace this:

Farmers grow crops.

2 Colour these:

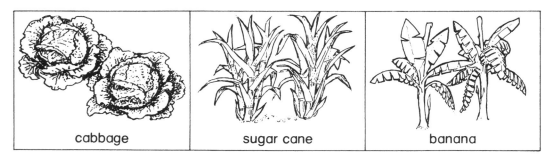

| cabbage | sugar cane | banana |

3 Trace this:

Farmers rear animals.

4 Colour these animals:

cow	fish	sheep	rabbits
pigs	fowls	ducks	

5 Trace these:

6 Colour these:

Planting seedlings	
Cutting sugar cane	
Milking cow	

7 Trace these: **8 Colour** these:

Bathing pigs	
Feeding chicks	

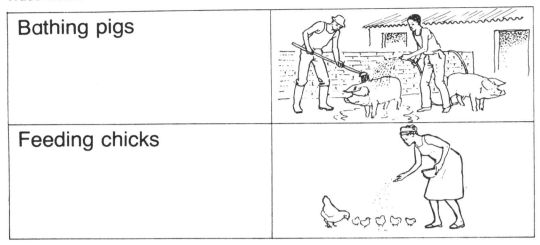

9 Do this:

Tell your class about more things that farmers do.

Plants

1 Trace this:

Plants are used for: food   flower gardens   medicine

building materials   clothing

2 Now **write** the uses of the plants below.   **3 Colour** the plants.

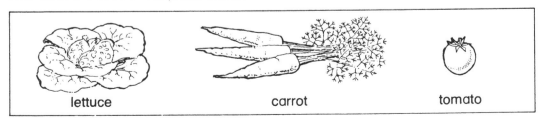

lettuce   carrot   tomato

These plants are used for f__ __d.

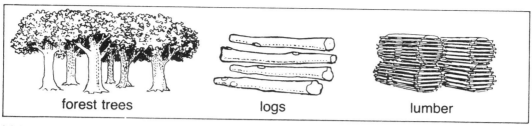

forest trees   logs   lumber

We get b___ld___g m__t__r___ls from these plants.

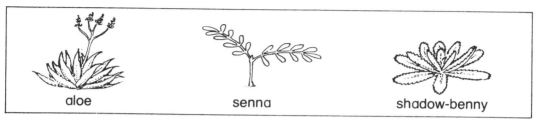

aloe   senna   shadow-benny

These plants are used for m__d__c___e.

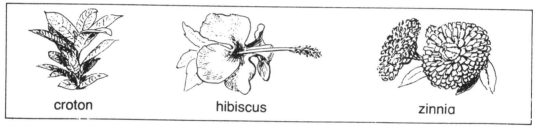

croton   hibiscus   zinnia

We use these plants in our fl__w__r g__rd_____.

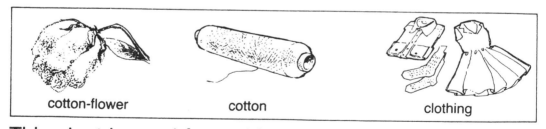

cotton-flower   cotton   clothing

This plant is used for making cl__th___g.

4 **Trace** and **read** this:

The parts of a plant are:

root   stem   leaf   flower   fruit   seed

5 Now **write** in the parts of the plant below.

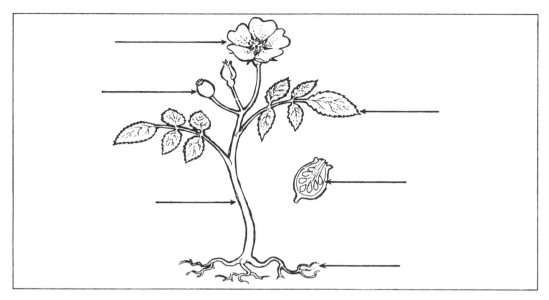

6 Colour the plant above.

Seeds, fruits and vegetables

1 Write these names under the pictures.

pineapple oranges mangoes cabbage corn ochroes beans carrots bananas

2 Colour the pictures.

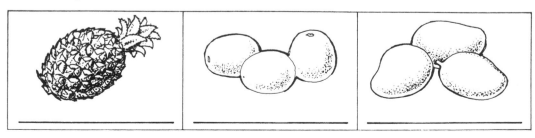

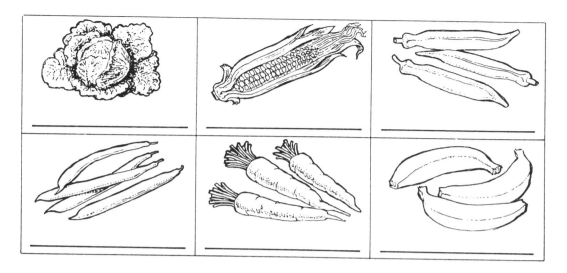

3 **Draw** and **colour** these:

a banana	a mango	a bean seed

4 Now **do** this:

Collect seeds, fruits and vegetables for your class Nature Corner.

New plants from old

1 **Trace** these:

seeds   cuttings   shoots

2 Now **write** the words in the spaces below:

We get new plants from s____d__.

We get new plants from c_____.

We get new plants from sh_____.

3 **Colour** these pictures and **trace** the names below them.

4 **Choose** the correct word (seeds, shoots, cuttings) and **write** it in the spaces below.

Bean plant	New bean plants grow from s_____
Sugar cane plants	We get new sugar cane plants from c_____
Rose plants	New rose plants grow from c_____
Banana plants	We get new banana plants from s_____

 Yam plants	New yam plants grow from c_____
 Corn plant	We get new corn plants from s_____

Animals around us

1 **Write** the names of these animals under the pictures below: dog fowl goat pig
cat sheep cow horse fish insect lizard snail centipede donkey squirrel

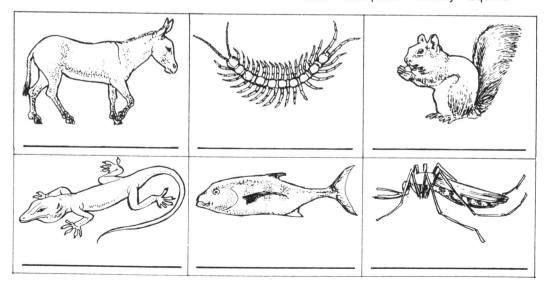

_____ _____ _____

_____ _____ _____

_____ _____ _____

2 From the list of animals on page 13, **draw, colour** and **name** these:

One pet animal	One work animal	We get eggs from this animal
_____	_____	_____
One animal from which we get meat	We get wool from this animal	We use this animal for sports (racing)
_____	_____	_____

Soil

1 Trace these:

Soil is found on the earth's surface.

Plants mainly grow in soil.

2 Look at the picture below and **find out** what soil contains.

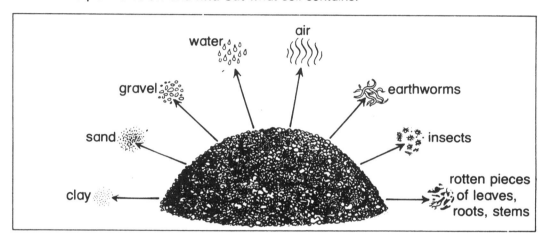

3 Now **write** below what soil contains.

_____

_____

_____

4 What makes soil rich?
Look at the pictures on the next page and **find** the answers.

manure   rich soil   fertiliser

5 Now **write** below what makes soil rich.

M_____ and f_____ make soil rich.

.

6 **Colour** these: **Trace** these:

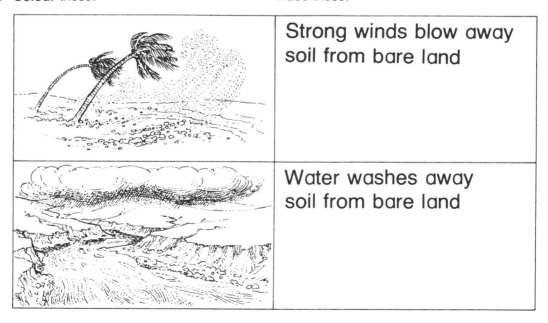

Strong winds blow away
soil from bare land

Water washes away
soil from bare land

7 How is soil saved?
  Look at the pictures and **find** the answers.

By digging good drains

By covering the land with dry grass

By planting grass

By planting trees

8 Now **write** below how soil is saved.

Soil is saved by:

1 _____

2 _____

3 _____

4 _____

9 Colour the pictures above.

Weather

These words tell us about the weather.

sunny   rainy   cloudy   windy

1 Now, **write** these words about the weather in the pictures below.

2 **Colour** the pictures.

It is _____

The weather is_____

Here it is _____

It is _____

3 **Trace**, this:

There are two seasons:

1. The dry season

2. The wet season

4 Look at these pictures.

Find out what happens in the dry season.

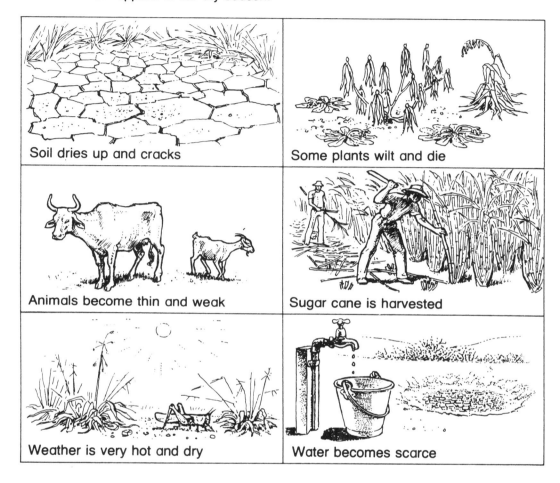

Soil dries up and cracks

Some plants wilt and die

Animals become thin and weak

Sugar cane is harvested

Weather is very hot and dry

Water becomes scarce

5 Colour the pictures about the dry season.

6 Now **write** below what happens in the dry season.

In the dry season:

1 _____

2 _____

3 _____

4 _____

5 _____

6 _____

7 Colour these pictures about the wet season.

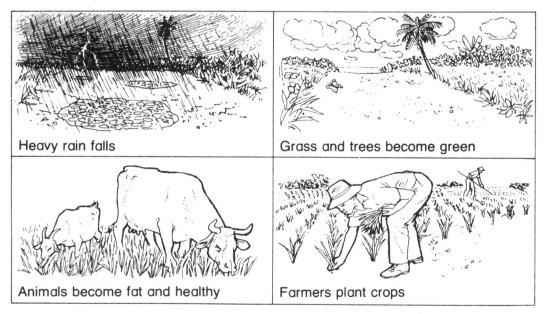

| Heavy rain falls | Grass and trees become green |
| Animals become fat and healthy | Farmers plant crops |

Tools and machines

1 Write these names under the pictures below: hoe cutlass fork water-can rake
trowel garden-line sprayer hand-fork spade milking-machine tractor

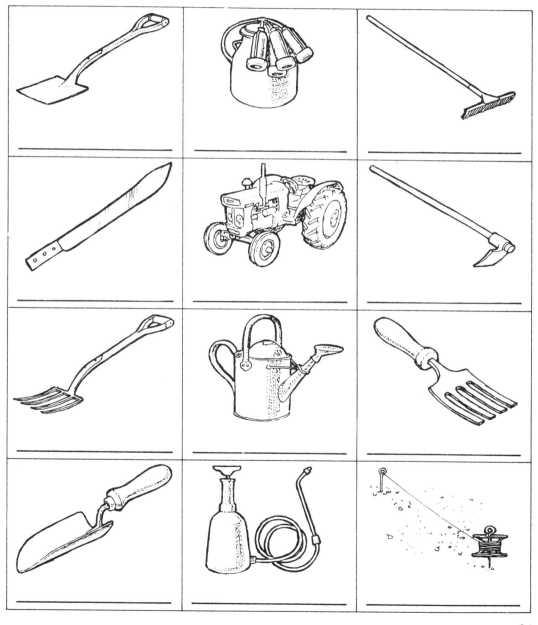

2 Draw and **colour** these tools

Tools for digging	Tools for cutting	Tools for draining

3 Look at the pictures and **write** what is taking place below each one.

Choose from this list:

storing tools

oiling tools

fitting handles to tools

sharpening tools

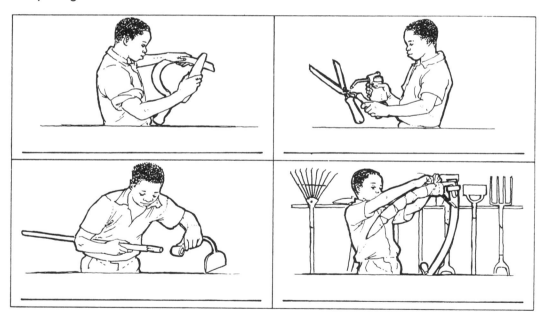

Growing crops

1 **Write** the names below the pictures below. Choose from this list:
cabbage cucumbers lettuce ochroes onions pumpkin tomatoes beans
corn melongene bananas sweet potato

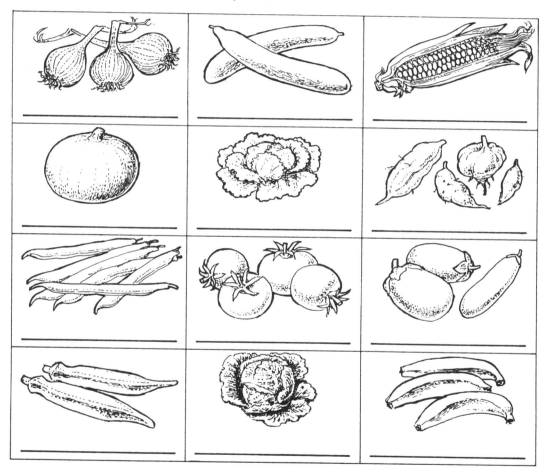

2 From the list of crops **write** the names of four (4) crops that you grow at home.

1 _____   2 _____

3 _____   4 _____

3 Now **write** the names of two (2) crops that you grow at school.

1_____ 2_____

4 **Draw** and **colour** these:

a banana	a carrot	an orange

5 **Look** at these pictures and **find out** how to grow a crop.

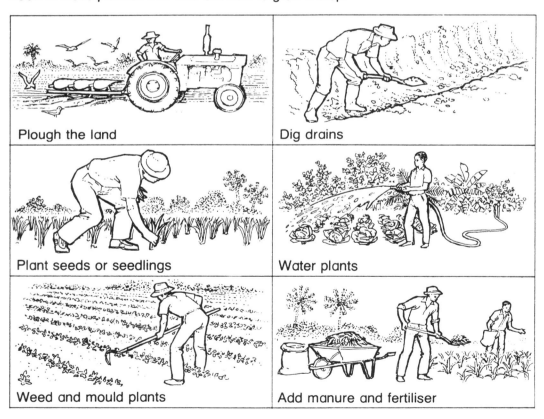

Plough the land

Dig drains

Plant seeds or seedlings

Water plants

Weed and mould plants

Add manure and fertiliser

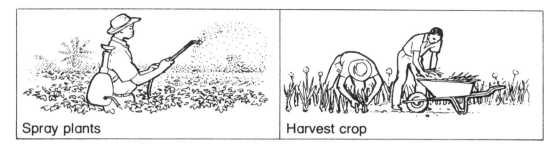

| Spray plants | Harvest crop |

6 Now **write** below all the things you must do to grow a crop.

1 _____

2 _____

3 _____

4 _____

5 _____

6 _____

7 _____

8 _____

Rearing animals

1 **Write** the names below the farm animals on the next page.
Choose from the list at the top of the next page.

goat kid cow calf hen chicks sow piglets donkey foal rabbit kittens
duck ducklings turkey poults

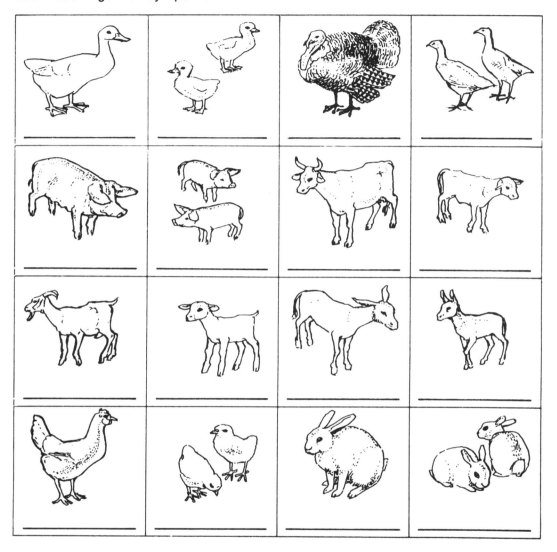

2 **Draw** and **colour** these:

a cock	a ram goat

3 Look at these pictures and **find out** how to take care of and manage farm animals. **Colour** the pictures.

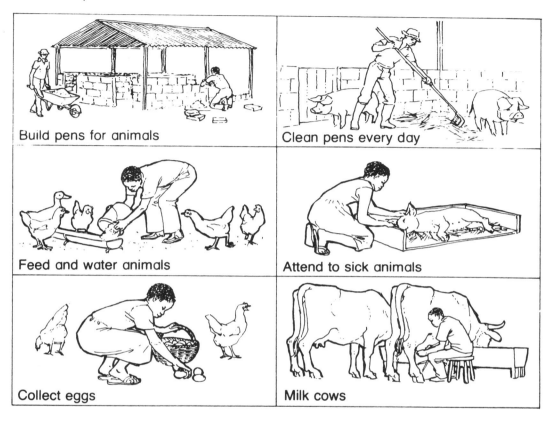

Build pens for animals

Clean pens every day

Feed and water animals

Attend to sick animals

Collect eggs

Milk cows

4 Now **write** below some of the things you must do to take care of and manage farm animals.

1 _____

2 _____

3 _____

4 _____

5 _____

6 _____

Friends and enemies of the farmer

1 **Trace** these:

Useful plants, animals and people are friends of the farmer. Harmful plants, animals and people are enemies of the farmer.

2 These are friends of the farmer. **Write** the name below each picture. **Choose** from this list.
bee   cow   fowl   frog   orange   policeman   coconut   ladybird   extension-officer   lizard

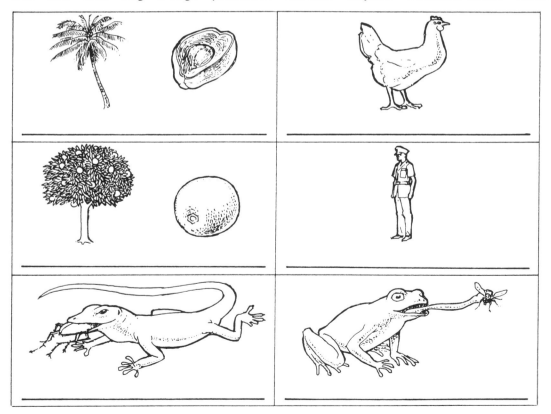

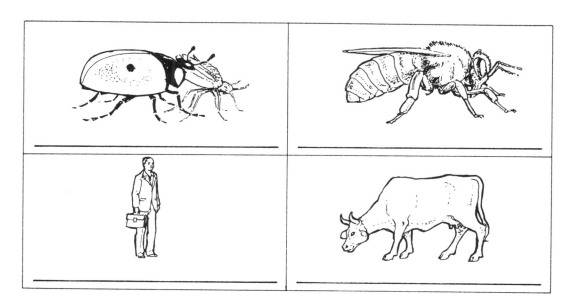

_____   _____

_____   _____

3 These are enemies of the farmer.

Write their names below the pictures. Choose from this list:

weeds   rats   mongoose   caterpillars   insects   vines   thieves
some birds   squirrel   ticks and lice

_____   _____

_____   _____

_____   _____

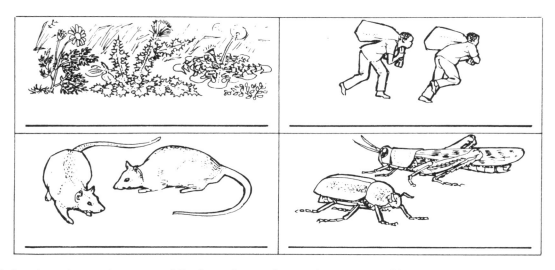

_____

4 **Look** at these pictures and **find out** how a farmer keeps away his enemies.
Colour the pictures.

Uprooting and hoeing weeds

Spraying weeds

Spraying insects

Trapping animals

Shooting animals

Reporting thieves to Police

Cutting out vines | Poisoning rats

5 Now **write** below how a farmer keeps away his enemies.

1 _____

2 _____

3 _____

4 _____

5 _____

6 _____

7 _____

8 _____

The market

Trace this:

People sell goods and buy goods in the market.

2 These goods are sold in the market.
Draw and **colour** them.

oranges	bananas	eggs
ochroes	fish	tomatoes
sweet potato	pumpkin	meat

3 **Colour** this picture.

a market